MY GOD AND KIN

FRANK COLQUHOUN is a former Canon Residentiary and Vice-Dean of Norwich Cathedral. Previously, most of his life was spent in South London, where he was for seven years Vicar of Wallington and later Canon and Chancellor of Southwark Cathedral and Principal of the Southwark Ordination Course. Now retired, he lives at Bexhill in Sussex.

His many books include *Parish Prayers*, *Contemporary Parish Prayers* and *New Parish Prayers*. He is also editor of the revised edition of the BBC service book, *New Every Morning*. His previous books for Triangle include *Family Prayers*, *Prayers for Today* and *Prayers for Everyone*.

My God and King

PRAYERS OF
CHRISTIAN DEVOTION

compiled and edited by

FRANK COLQUHOUN

First published 1993
Triangle
SPCK
Holy Trinity Church
Marylebone Road
London NW1 4DU

British Library Cataloguing in Publication Data
A catalogue record for this book is available from the British Library.
ISBN 0-281-04706-5

Photoset by
Rowland Phototypesetting Ltd, Bury St Edmunds, Suffolk
Printed and bound in Great Britain by
BPCC Paperbacks Ltd
Member of BPCC Ltd

CONTENTS

PREFACE

The distinctive feature of the prayers I have put together in this book is their devotional character. They are not general prayers for general use. They are directly related to the spiritual life of the Christian believer.

But this, let me add, does not mean that they are all very much alike. There is considerable variety in the prayers. They come from different sources, different ages, different authors, different backgrounds. A glance at the Contents list will make this clear.

One further comment. I hope that the prayers, wisely used, may not only deepen the reader's spiritual life, but that those who use them may also be better fitted for their everyday life in the service of their God and King.

Frank Colquhoun
Bexhill, 1993

ACKNOWLEDGEMENTS

The prayers based on the writings of Julian of Norwich are from *Praying with the English Mystics*, edited by Jenny Robertson and published by Triangle, and are reprinted by permission.

The Collects from The Book of Common Prayer (1662), the rights of which are vested in the Crown in perpetuity within the United Kingdom, are reproduced by permission of Cambridge University Press, Her Majesty's Printers.

Part One

PRAISE AND
WORSHIP

ADORATION OF THE TRINITY

I

Worthy of praise from every mouth,
of worship from every creature,
is thy glorious name,
O Father, Son and Holy Spirit,
Who didst create the world by the word of thy power,
    and in love didst wonderfully redeem it.
Wherefore with angels and archangels,
    and with all the company of heaven,
we adore and magnify thy name,
through Jesus Christ our Lord.

Nestorian Liturgy (6th century)

We praise thee, O God,
    we acknowledge thee to be the Lord,
All the earth doth worship thee,
    the Father everlasting.
To thee all angels cry aloud,
    the heavens and all the powers therein,
To thee cherubim and seraphim
    continually do cry,
Holy, Holy, Holy, God of power and might.
Heaven and earth are full of the majesty of thy glory.

Te Deum Laudamus (5th century)

3

Almighty God, most blessed and most holy,
before the brightness of whose presence
   the angels veil their faces:
with lowly reverence and adoring love
   we acknowledge thine eternal glory,
   and worship thee,
Father, Son and Holy Spirit,
   eternal Trinity.
Blessing and honour, glory and power,
be unto our God, for ever and ever.

Book of Common Order

4

Glory be to God in the highest,
  Lord of heaven and earth,
who so loved the world
  as to send his only Son
to redeem us from sin,
  and to obtain for us everlasting life.
All praise be thine, most gracious God,
  for thine infinite mercies towards us
  in Jesus Christ our Lord.

Archbishop Hamilton (1511–1571)

5

Almighty God, you are the King of Glory:
    you rule the world in your Majesty.
Humbly we yield you
    our homage and allegiance.
Gladly we offer you
    our worship and adoration.
You are worthy of endless praise,
    for yours is the kingdom,
    the power and the glory,
    for ever.

                                        F.C.

6

Holy, holy, holy Lord,
    God of power and might,
heaven and earth are full of your glory.
    Hosanna in the highest.

Tersanctus

7

To him who loves us, and has freed us from our sins by
his blood, and made us a kingdom, priests to serve his
God and Father: to him be glory and dominion for ever
and ever! Amen.

Revelation 1.5,6

Part Two

DEVOTIONAL PRAYERS
OLD AND NEW

PERSONAL PRAYERS

8   *The will of God*

O Lord, my God, your will is holy, loving and wise.
    Let your will be done in me, for me,
        through me, in spite of me;
for the sake of him whose greatest joy was to do
your will, even Jesus Christ our Lord.

George Appleton

9   *Only love*

O God of mercy,
the giver of all good things,
keep the door of my heart,
    that only love may enter therein;
and of my lips,
    that only love may speak through them;
for Jesus Christ's sake.

Daily Prayer

10 Love's response

Thank you, my Father, for your love and all you have done for me.

Help me to do more for you, to live only and always for your glory;

through Jesus Christ my Lord.

F.C.

11 Forgiven much

O merciful God, I have been forgiven much and I want to love you much.

Let me day by day realise the depth of sin from which you have rescued me, and the kingdom of love into which you have brought me through your beloved Son, Jesus Christ my Lord and Saviour.

George Appleton

Heavenly Father, give me the faith
  to commit my life to you
  without question or reserve;
that, trusting only and wholly
  to your love and wisdom,
I may meet all that life may bring
  with serenity and courage;
through the grace of Christ my Lord.

F.C.

13 *Close to Christ*

Lord, keep me ever near to you.

Let nothing separate me from you, let nothing keep me back from you.

If I fall, bring me back quickly to you, and make me hope in you, trust in you, and love you everlastingly.

E. B. Pusey (1800–1882)

14 *Father of mercies*

Most merciful Father,
    give me your grace to pardon me,
    your peace to quieten me,
    your joy to gladden me,
    your power to strengthen me,
      now and always.

F.C.

15 *All for Jesus*

Lord Jesus Christ, as I think of
    all you have done for me,
    all you have given me,
    all you have suffered for me,
help me by your grace to become
    all that you want me to be.

Adapted

CORPORATE PRAYERS

16   *The meaning of love*

Lord Jesus, you have taught us that love is the fulfilling of the law.

Teach us now what love really is, how much it costs, how deep it digs into our selfish lives.

Then give us the courage and the generosity to accept what this means today and tomorrow and in the whole future of our lives.

Michael Hollings

Heavenly Father,
may your love so fill our lives
that we may count
    nothing too small to do for you,
    nothing too much to give to you,
    and nothing too much to bear for you,
in the name and faith of your Son
Jesus Christ our Lord.

Adapted

18   *For a quiet mind*

O Lord, this is our desire, to walk along the appointed path of life in steadfastness of faith and in lowliness of heart.

Let not the cares or duties of this life press on us too heavily, but lighten the burden, that we may follow thy way in quietness, filled with thankfulness for all thy mercies; through Jesus Christ our Lord.

Maria Hare (1782–1870)

19 Pentecost

O God, we pray that as the Holy Spirit came in wind and fire to the apostles at Pentecost, so he may come to us now, breathing new life into our souls and kindling in our hearts the flame of love; through Jesus Christ our Lord.

F.C.

20 Think on these things

Heavenly Father, may your indwelling Holy Spirit so fill and possess our souls that he may deliver us from all evil and unclean thoughts, and ever direct our minds to whatever things are true and honourable, just and pure, lovely and gracious, and all things worthy of praise, as revealed in your Son Jesus Christ our Lord.

Derived from Philippians 4.8

21   *Darkness and light*

In darkness and in light,
in trouble and in joy,
help us, heavenly Father,
   to trust your love,
   to serve your purpose,
   and to praise your name;
through Jesus Christ our Lord.

     A prayer from New Zealand

22   *Christian joy*

God of hope,
fill us with all joy and peace in our faith,
   that we may serve you with gladness,
   delight to do your will,
   and always make melody to you in our hearts;
through Jesus Christ our Lord.

     F.C.

23 *For humility*

God our Father,
give us a humble and contrite heart,
and deliver us from pride and self-glory.
In all our doings teach us
    to think less of ourselves,
    more of others,
    and most of all of you,
our God and Saviour,
    to whom alone be all praise and glory.

F.C.

24 For a lively faith

Let us not rest, O Lord, in a dead, ineffectual faith, but grant that it may be such as may show itself in good works, enabling us to overcome the world and to conform to the image of the Christ in whom we believe; for his name's sake.

Joseph Addison (1672–1719)

25 Pilgrims' progress

Lord God, help us to travel forward in our lives with you, not becoming stuck in the past, but rather, trusting in your love and your promises, may we move on in the ever new life you give us in your Son Jesus Christ our Lord.

Richard Morgan

26   The dedicated life

Lord, help us by your grace to fulfil the purpose for which in your wisdom you created us and in your love redeemed us; that our days on earth may be of service to others and accomplish something of worth for you and your kingdom.

F.C.

27   Glory be to God on high

The God and Father of our Lord Jesus Christ so open our eyes that we may see that blessed hope to which we are called, and that we may glorify the only true God and Jesus Christ, whom he sent down to us from heaven; to whom with the Father and the Holy Spirit be rendered all honour and glory to all eternity.

John Jewel (1522–1571)

Part Three

PRAYERS FROM
THE PSALMS
OF THE
OLD TESTAMENT

28   *The penitent sinner*

Have mercy on me, O God,
   according to thy loving kindness,
according to thy abundant mercy
   blot out my transgressions.
For I acknowledge my transgressions,
   and my sin is ever before me.
Hide thy face from my sins,
   and blot out all my misdeeds.
Create in me a clean heart, O God,
   and renew a steadfast spirit within me.
The sacrifices acceptable to God
   are a broken spirit;
a broken and contrite heart, O God,
   thou wilt not despise.

Psalm 51. 1–3, 9, 10, 17

29 *The trusting soul*

To thee, O Lord, I lift up my heart,
   my God, I trust in thee,
    let me not be put to shame.
Show me thy ways, O Lord,
   and teach me thy paths.
Lead me in thy truth, and teach me,
   For thou art the God of my salvation.
Be merciful, O Lord, of thy tender mercy
   and steadfast love,
    for they have been ever of old.

Psalm 25.1, 4–6

O Lord, our Lord,
　　how majestic is thy name
　　in all the earth!
When I consider thy heavens,
　　the work of thy fingers,
the moon and the stars
　　which thou hast established;
what is man,
　　that thou art mindful of him,
the son of man,
　　that thou dost care for him?
Yet thou has made him
　　little less than God,
and crowned him with glory and honour.

Psalm 8. 1, 3–5

31 *De profundis*

Out of the depths I cry to thee, O Lord!
   O Lord, hear my voice!
Let thy ears be attentive to my supplications.
If thou, Lord, shouldest keep a record of our sin,
   who then could stand?
But there is forgiveness with thee,
   that thou mayest be feared.

Psalm 130. 1–4

32 *In the morning*

Lord, let me hear of thy steadfast love
    in the morning,
      for in thee have I put my trust.
Show me the way I should go,
      for to thee I lift up my soul.
Teach me to do thy will,
      for thou art my God.

Psalm 143.8, 10

33   *God of the nations*

May God be gracious to us and bless us,
    and make his face to shine upon us,
that thy way may be known on earth,
    thy saving power among all nations.
Let the peoples praise thee, O God;
    let all the peoples praise thee!
Let the nations be glad and sing for joy,
    for thou dost rule the peoples justly,
    and guide the nations upon earth.

Psalm 67. 1–4

All-seeing God

Lord, thou hast searched me and known me!
Thou knowest my sitting down and rising up,
  thou discernest my thoughts from afar.
Such knowledge is too wonderful for me,
  so high that I cannot attain it.
. . .

Search me, O God, and know my heart!
  Try me and know my thoughts!
See if there is any wicked way in me,
  and lead me in the way everlasting.

Psalm 139.1, 6, 23–4

35   *Our God reigns*

The Lord is king, he is robed in majesty
  and girded with strength.
Thy throne is established from of old;
  thou art from everlasting.
O Lord, the floods lift up their voice,
  the floods lift up their roaring.
The Lord reigns supreme in heaven,
  mightier than the thunder of great waters.
Thy law stands firm, O Lord;
  holiness adorns thy house for evermore.

                                              Psalm 93

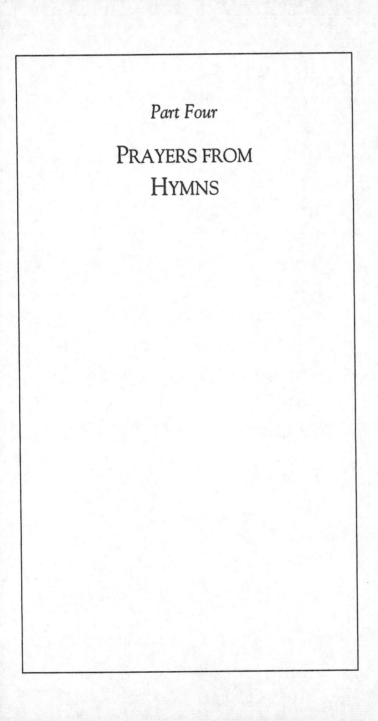

Part Four

PRAYERS FROM HYMNS

A life of praise

Fill thou my life, O Lord my God,
   In every part with praise,
That my whole being may proclaim
   Thy being and thy ways.

Not for the lip of praise alone,
   Nor e'en the praising heart
I ask, but for a life made up
   Of praise in every part.

      · · ·

So shall no part of day or night
   From sacredness be free,
But all my life, in every step,
   Be fellowship with thee.

      Horatius Bonar (1808–1882)

37 Celestial fire

O thou who camest from above
　The pure, celestial fire to impart,
Kindle a flame of sacred love
　On the mean altar of my heart.

There let it for thy glory burn
　With inextinguishable blaze,
And trembling to its source return
　In humble prayer and fervent praise.

Jesus, confirm my heart's desire
　To work, and speak, and think for thee.
Still let me guard the holy fire,
　And still stir up thy gift in me.

Charles Wesley (1707–1788)

38 *Christ within me*

May the mind of Christ my Saviour
   Live in me from day to day,
By his love and power controlling
   All I do and say.

May the word of God dwell richly
   In my heart from hour to hour,
So that all may see I triumph
   Only through his power.

May the love of Jesus fill me
   As the waters fill the sea;
Him exalting, self abasing,
   This is victory.

      Kate B. Wilkinson (1859–1928)

39   *The appeal of the Cross*

O my Saviour, lifted
    From the earth for me,
Draw me in thy mercy
    Nearer unto thee.

Lift my earth-bound longings,
    Fix them, Lord, above;
Draw me with the magnet
    Of thy mighty love.

And I come, Lord Jesus,
    Dare I turn away?
No, thy love hath conquered,
    And I come today.
  W. Walsham How (1823–1897)

40 *Immeasurable grace*

Come, dearest Lord, descend and dwell
By faith and love in every breast;
Then shall we know and taste and feel
The joys that cannot be expressed.

Come, fill our hearts with inward strength;
Make our enlargèd souls possess
And learn the height and breadth and length
Of thine immeasurable grace.

Isaac Watts (1674–1748)

41   *Growing in grace*

O Jesus Christ, grow thou in me,
    And all things else recede;
My heart be daily nearer thee,
    From sin be daily freed.

. . .

Fill me with gladness from above,
    Hold me by strength divine;
Lord, let the glow of thy great love
    Through my whole being shine.

Make this poor self grow less and less,
    Be thou my life and aim;
Oh, make me daily, through thy grace,
    More meet to bear thy name.

J. C. Lavater (1741–1801)
trs. Elizabeth Lee-Smith

42   The unseen Christ

Jesus, these eyes have never seen
   That radiant form of thine;
The veil of sense hangs dark between
   Thy blessèd face and mine.

Yet, though I have not seen, and still
   Must rest in faith alone,
I love thee, dearest Lord, and will,
   Unseen but not unknown.

               Ray Palmer (1808–1887)

Invocation of the Spirit

Breathe on me, Breath of God;
    Fill me with life anew,
That I may love what thou dost love,
    And do what thou wouldst do.

. . .

Breathe on me, Breath of God,
    Till I am wholly thine,
Until this earthly part of me
    Glows with thy fire divine.

Breathe on me, Breath of God,
    So shall I never die,
But live with thee the perfect life
    Of thine eternity.
           Edwin Hatch (1835–1889)

Lord, it belongs not to my care
   Whether I die or live;
To love and serve thee is my share,
   And this thy grace must give.

If life be long, I will be glad
   That I may long obey;
If short, yet why should I be sad
   To soar to endless day?

Come, Lord, when grace has made me meet
   Thy blessed face to see;
For if thy work on earth be sweet,
   What will thy glory be!

               Richard Baxter (1615–1691)

Part Five

COLLECTS FROM
THE BOOK OF
COMMON PRAYER

45　For God's peace

Almighty and everlasting God,
   who dost govern all things
   in heaven and earth,
mercifully hear the supplications
   of thy people,
and grant us thy peace
   all the days of our life;
through Jesus Christ our Lord.

The Second Sunday after Epiphany

O Lord, who hast taught us
   that all our doings without charity
   are nothing worth:
Send thy Holy Ghost,
   and pour into our hearts
   that most excellent gift of charity,
   the very bond of peace and of all virtues,
   without which whosoever liveth
   is counted dead before thee:
Grant this for thine only Son
   Jesus Christ's sake.

Quinquagesima Sunday

47 *Things temporal and eternal*

O God, the protector of all that trust in thee,
    without whom nothing is strong,
    nothing is holy:
Increase and multiply upon us thy mercy;
that, thou being our ruler and guide,
    we may so pass through things temporal,
    that we finally lose not the things eternal:
Grant this, O heavenly Father,
    for Jesus Christ's sake our Lord.

The Fourth Sunday after Trinity

48   *Love for God*

O God, who hast prepared for them that love thee
    such good things as pass man's understanding:
Pour into our hearts such love toward thee,
that we, loving thee above all things,
    may obtain thy promises,
    which exceed all that we can desire;
through Jesus Christ our Lord.

The Sixth Sunday after Trinity

Lord of all power and might,
     who art the author and giver of all good things:
Graft in our hearts the love of thy name,
     increase in us true religion,
     nourish us with all goodness,
     and of thy great mercy keep us in the same;
through Jesus Christ our Lord.

The Seventh Sunday after Trinity

Grant to us, Lord, we beseech thee,
   the spirit to think and do always
   such things as be rightful;
that we, who cannot do anything
   that is good without thee,
   may by thee be enabled to live
   according to thy will;
through Jesus Christ our Lord.

     The Ninth Sunday after Trinity

51 *Life in the Spirit*

O God, forasmuch as without thee
    we are not able to please thee;
Mercifully grant that thy Holy Spirit
    may in all things direct and rule our hearts;
through Jesus Christ our Lord.

The Nineteenth Sunday after Trinity

52 *Pardon and peace*

Grant, we beseech thee, merciful Lord,
    to thy faithful people pardon and peace;
that they may be cleansed from all their sins,
    and serve thee with a quiet mind;
through Jesus Christ our Lord.

The Twenty-First Sunday after Trinity

53 *Go before us, O Lord*

Prevent us, O Lord, in all our doings
   with thy most gracious favour,
   and further us with thy continual help;
that in all our works,
   begun, continued, and ended in thee,
   we may glorify thy holy Name,
   and finally by thy mercy
   obtain everlasting life;
through Jesus Christ our Lord.

Post Communion prayer

Part Six

PRAYERS FROM
THE NEW TESTAMENT

Adapted from the letters of St Paul
and other writers

54 For mutual love

May the Lord make you increase and abound in love to one another and to all men, just as we do to you, so that he may establish your hearts unblameable in holiness before our God and Father, at the coming of our Lord Jesus with all his saints.

1 Thessalonians 3.12, 13

55 For sanctification

May the God of peace himself sanctify you wholly; and may your whole spirit, soul and body be kept sound and blameless at the coming of our Lord Jesus Christ. He who calls you is faithful, and he will do it.

1 Thessalonians 5.23, 24

56   The indwelling Christ

I bow in prayer before the Father, from whom every family in heaven and on earth takes its name, that out of the riches of his glory he may grant you to be strengthened with power through his Spirit in your inner being, so that Christ may dwell in your hearts through faith.

Ephesians 3. 14–17

57   Immeasurable love

I pray for you, that being rooted and grounded in love you may have power to comprehend with all the saints what is the breadth and length and height and depth of the love of Christ, which surpasses knowledge, that you may be filled with all the fullness of God.

Ephesians 3. 17–19

58 *For discerning love*

It is my prayer that your love may abound more and more, with knowledge and true judgement, so that you may discern what is best, and may be pure and without blame until the day of Christ, filled with the fruits of righteousness, to the glory and praise of God.

Philippians 1.9–11

59 *A life worthy of the Lord*

We have never ceased praying for you and asking God to fill you with the knowledge of his will in all spiritual wisdom and understanding, so that you may lead a life worthy of the Lord, fully pleasing to him, bearing fruit in every good work and increasing in the knowledge of God.

Colossians 1.9, 10

60   *Equipped for service*

May the God of peace, who raised from the dead our Lord Jesus, the great shepherd of the sheep, equip you with everything good for the doing of his will, working in you that which is pleasing in his sight; through Jesus Christ, to whom be glory for ever and ever. Amen.

Hebrews 13.20–21

61 Benediction

May the grace of our Lord Jesus Christ,
and the love of God,
and the fellowship of the Holy Spirit,
be with you all.

2 Corinthians 13.14

62 Doxology

Now to him who is able to keep you from falling,
and to present you before his glorious presence
    without fault and with great joy:
to the only God, our Saviour,
be glory, majesty, dominion and power,
through Jesus Christ our Lord,
    now and for evermore. Amen.

Jude 24–5

Part Seven

PRAYERS OF
A CHRISTIAN POET

Christina Rossetti (1830–1894)

63   The mind of Christ

Eternal God, let this mind be in us which was also in Christ Jesus; that as he from his loftiness stooped to the death of the cross, so we in our lowliness may humble ourselves, believing, obeying, living and dying, for his name's sake.

64   The spirit of praise

Lord Jesus Christ,
Wisdom and Word of God,
so fill us with thy most Holy Spirit,
that out of the abundance of our hearts
our mouths may speak thy praise,
in psalms and hymns and spiritual songs,
to thy everlasting glory.

65   Contentment

O Lord, whose way is perfect,
help us always to trust in thy goodness;
   that walking with thee
   and following thee in all simplicity,
we may possess quiet and contented minds,
   and may cast all our care on thee
   who carest for us;
for thy dear Son's sake, Jesus Christ.

66 *Fellowship with the saints*

Lord, make us like-minded with all saints,
    whether on earth or in heaven;
that we may worship thee as they worship,
    trust thee as they trust,
    and love thee as they love;
for the sake of our Saviour Jesus Christ.

67 Our hiding-place

O Lord, our hiding-place, grant us wisdom to seek no
hiding-place out of thee in life or in death.

Hide us in thine own presence from the provoking of
men; keep us from the strife of tongues; and teach us to
seek peace and pursue it; for thy name's sake.

68 Fear and love

Teach us, Lord, to fear thee
   without being afraid;
to fear thee in love,
   that we may love without fear;
through Jesus Christ our Lord.

69 *Forgiven and forgiving*

O Lord, because we often sin
   and have to ask for pardon,
help us to forgive
   as we would be forgiven:
neither mentioning old offences
   committed against us,
nor dwelling upon them in thought,
but loving our brother freely
   as thou freely lovest us;
for thy name's sake.

70 *Time and eternity*

O God of time and eternity,
  who makest us creatures of time,
that when time is over,
  we may attain thy blessed eternity:
with time thy gift
  give us also wisdom to redeem the time,
  lest our day of grace be lost;
for our Lord Jesus' sake.

71 *Love*

Almighty God and Father,
   by whom and before whom
   we are all brethren,
grant us so truly to love one another
   that evidently and beyond all doubt
   we may love thee;
through Jesus Christ, our Lord and brother.

Part Eight

PRAYERS OF
AN ENGLISH MYSTIC

Based on the writings of
Dame Julian of Norwich (c. 1342–after 1413)

God, of your goodness,
    give me yourself,
for you are sufficient for me.
I can ask nothing less
    to be worthy of you;
and if I asked anything less
    I should always be in want.
In you alone do I have all.

73 *Purity of heart*

To you, O God,
    every heart is open,
    from you no secret is hidden.
Purify my mind,
    my thoughts and my heart,
    with the gift of your grace,
so that I may love you perfectly
    and praise you worthily.

74 *Enfolded in love*

Lord, you are everything that is good
    and for our comfort.
You are our clothing;
you wrap and enfold us for love.
You surround us with your love,
    which is so tender
that you may never forsake us.

Blessed be you, O Lord,
who always were, and are,
   and ever shall be:
almighty, all wisdom, all love.
Everything you have made,
heaven and earth and all creation,
   is great and generous,
   beautiful and good;
for you created everything for love,
   and by your love it is preserved.

76 *You desire to possess us*

God, our lover, you desire us
    to adhere to you with all our power,
and you want us always
    to adhere to your goodness
    with all the heart can conceive.
This pleases you most,
and soonest profits the soul
    so preciously loved.

77 *The love of Christ*

Lord Jesus, how much you love me!
You loved me so much
  before you died for me.
And now you have died for me,
and willingly suffered what you could.
So now all your bitter pain and labour
is turned into everlasting joy and bliss,
  for me and for you.

78 *Jesus our true Mother*

Jesus, by our first creation
  you are our true Mother in nature,
and by taking our created nature
  you are our true Mother in grace.
All the sweet and loving offices
of beloved motherhood
are appropriated to you,
  whole and safe for evermore.

79 *Love was your meaning*

Lord, you said,
What do you wish to know
    of your Lord's meaning in this thing?
And I said, I know it well, Lord,
    that love was your meaning.
Who revealed it to me?
    Love.
Why do you reveal it to me?
    For love.
Lord, let me remain in this,
and I will know more,
    and know no different for ever.

God, you are Trinity:
  Trinity is our maker,
  Trinity is our protector,
  Trinity is our everlasting lover,
  Trinity is our endless joy
  and our bliss,
by our Lord Jesus Christ,
and in our Lord Jesus Christ.

Part Nine

PRAYERS OF THE
CHURCH'S SAINTS

through the centuries

PRAYER OF ST TERESA

CHRIST

*has no
body now on earth but
yours,
no hands but yours.*

*Yours are the eyes through
which must look out
Christ's
compassion on the world.*

*Yours are the feet with
which
He is to go about doing
good.*

*Yours are the hands with
which
He is to bless people now.*

81

Almighty God, who hast made us for thyself,
so that our hearts are restless till they find rest in
thee:
grant us purity of heart and strength of purpose,
that nothing may hinder us from knowing thy will,
no weakness from doing it,
but that in thy service we may find our perfect
freedom;
through Jesus Christ our Lord.

St Augustine (5th century)

Breathe in us Holy Spirit
that we may think what is holy
Move in us Holy Spirit
that we may do what is holy
Attract us Holy Spirit
that we may life what is holy
Strengthen us Holy Spirit
That we may nourish what is holy
Guard us Holy Spirit
that we may keep what is holy
(St. Augustine of Canterbury)

May the strength of God pilot us,
may the power of God preserve us,
may the wisdom of God instruct us,
may the hand of God protect us,
may the way of God direct us,
may the shield of God defend us,
may the host of God guard us.
  May Christ be with us,
  Christ before us,
  Christ in us,
  Christ over us,
this day and for evermore.

  St Patrick's Breastplate (5th century)

83

O gracious God and Father,
   give us wisdom to perceive thee,
   diligence to seek thee,
   patience to wait for thee,
   a heart to meditate upon thee,
   and a life to proclaim thee,
for thy honour and glory.

St Benedict (6th century)

84

Eternal God, the refuge of all thy children,
    in our weakness thou art our strength,
    in our darkness our light,
    in our sorrow our comfort and peace.
May we live as ever in thy presence,
and serve thee in our daily lives;
through Jesus Christ our Lord.

                    St Boniface (7th century)

85

O Lord our God,
grant us grace to desire thee with our whole heart;
    that so desiring thee we may seek and find thee,
    and so finding thee we may love thee,
    and loving thee may hate those sins
        from which thou hast redeemed us;
through our Lord Jesus Christ.

St Anselm (12th century)

86

Lord, make us instruments of thy peace,
    Where there is hatred, let us sow love;
    where there is injury, pardon;
    where there is doubt, faith;
    where there is despair, hope;
    where there is darkness, light;
    where there is sadness, joy.
O Divine Master, grant that we may
      not so much seek
    to be consoled as to console,
    to be understood as to understand,
    to be loved as to love.
For it is in giving that we receive,
    in pardoning that we are pardoned,
    and in dying that we are born to eternal life.

Commonly attributed to
St Francis of Assisi (13th century)

Thanks be to thee, my Lord Jesus Christ,
   for all the benefits thou hast won for me,
   for all the pains and insults thou hast
     borne for me,
O most merciful Redeemer, Friend and Brother,
   may I know thee more clearly,
   love thee more dearly,
   and follow thee more nearly,
day by day.

St Richard of Chichester (1197–1253)

88

Remember, O Lord, that thou art the God of mercy:
   have mercy on this poor sinner.
Look down, O Lord, on my longing heart
   and on my prayers which I address to thee;
and for thy name's sake forgive what I have done amiss.

                       St Teresa of Avila (1515–1582)

89

Teach us, good Lord, to serve thee as thou deservest:
   to give, and not to count the cost;
   to fight, and not to heed the wounds;
   to toil, and not to seek for rest;
   to labour, and not to ask for any reward,
save that of knowing that we do thy will.

                     St Ignatius Loyola (1491–1556)

Part Ten

SELECTED PASSAGES
FOR MEDITATION

'Be still, and know that I am God.'

90 The transcendence of God

God is what thought cannot better;
God is whom thought cannot reach;
God no thinking can even conceive.
Without God, man can have no being, no reason,
   no knowledge, no good desire, naught.
Thou, O God, art what thou art, transcending all.

Eric Milner-White (1884–1963)

91 *God and myself*

God created me: I belong to him.
I am a creature of God: I depend on him.
I am made in the image of God.
I will try to live after the example of Jesus Christ,
   the perfect image of God.

George Appleton

92   *Gain and loss*

Teach me, dear Lord, frequently to consider
   this truth:
That if I gain the whole world and lose you,
   I have lost everything;
whereas if I lose the world and gain you,
   in the end I have lost nothing.

John Henry Newman (1801–1890)

Worship is the submission of all our nature to God:
   the quickening of conscience by his holiness,
   the purifying of the imagination by his beauty;
   the opening of the heart to his love;
and all of this gathered up in adoration, the most selfless emotion of which we are capable, and therefore the chief remedy of that self-centredness which is our original sin.

William Temple (1881–1944)

When we say, 'The Lord's will be done', we often say it with a sigh, as though to submit to the Lord's will were a heavy, bitter trial.

Yet how inconsistent that is with all we know of God. If we really believe he is our Father, who loves and cares for his children, we should have no difficulty in believing that his will for us is the best thing that can possibly happen.

Robert Woods Colquhoun (1857–1940)

Let us not seek *out* of thee, O Lord, what we can find
only *in* thee: peace and rest and joy and bliss.

    Lift up our souls above the weary round of harassing
thoughts to the pure, serene atmosphere of thy
presence,

    that there we may breathe freely,

    there repose in thy love,

    there be at rest from ourselves;

and thence return arrayed with thy peace, to do and
bear what shall best please thee.

E. B. Pusey (1800–1882)

96   *Our care*

Cast all your care on him,
For he cares about you. (1 Peter 5.7)

O Lord, how happy should we be
If we could cast our care on thee,
   If we from self could rest;
And feel at heart that one above,
In perfect wisdom, perfect love,
   Is working for the best.

Joseph Anstice (1808–1836)

What God commands us is to believe in his Son Jesus Christ and to love one another.

This is how we know what love is: that Christ laid down his life for us. And we too ought to lay down our lives for our brothers.

My children, love must not be a matter of words or talk. It must be genuine and show itself in action.

From 1 John 3

98 *God within*

God be in my head,
   and in my understanding;
God be in my eyes,
   and in my looking;
God be in my mouth,
   and in my speaking;
God be in my heart,
   and in my thinking;
God be at my end,
   and at my departing.

     A Book of Hours (1514)

Whenever we come to the Lord in prayer, we do so in the assurance that he is present with us.

We do not have to seek his presence.

We are daily living in his presence.

So in our moments of prayer we may know that we are speaking to one who is near and not far off, whose love is all around us and who understands our every need.

And more: if in the stillness of our hearts we listen to him, we shall also hear him speaking to us.

F.C.

The prayer may be regarded as a series of word pictures, illustrating our relationship with God:

The loving child – *Our Father who art in heaven*
The devout worshipper – *Hallowed be thy name*
The loyal citizen – *Thy kingdom come*
The obedient servant – *Thy will be done*
The needy beggar – *Give us this day our daily bread*
The discharged debtor – *Forgive us our trespasses (debts)*
The vigilant pilgrim – *Lead us not into temptation*
The liberated captive – *Deliver us from evil.*

Anon

INDEX OF PRINCIPAL SUBJECTS

References are to numbered prayers

INDEX OF SOURCES

References are to numbered prayers

Also by Frank Colquhoun
and published by

Tri∧ngle

PRAYERS FOR TODAY

A modern book of prayers dealing with matters of
common experience. Divided into three sections, the
prayers cover personal life, the Christian pilgrimage and
a broad range of public issues. Many of the prayers are
also suitable for use in church or group worship.

PRAYERS FOR EVERYONE

A wide-ranging collection offering prayers for many
different situations. Prayers of Christian faith and
devotion are gathered together with some for everyday
needs and others showing a concern for the world
around us. The book also includes a special section of
Celtic material.

FAMILY PRAYERS

Prayers and thanksgivings for all family occasions – from
times of joy or of sadness; of celebration or of change;
from the birth of a new baby to the loss of a
grandparent. There are also prayers for friends,
neighbours, the local community and the
church fellowship.

Also available from
TriAngle

The PRAYING WITH series
A series of books making accessible the words of some of
the great characters and traditions of faith for use by all
Christians. There are 14 titles in the series, including:

PRAYING WITH HIGHLAND CHRISTIANS
Introduction by Sally Magnusson

PRAYING WITH SAINT TERESA
Introduction by Elaine Storkey

PRAYING WITH THE ORTHODOX TRADITION
Preface by Kallistos Ware

PRAYING WITH THE ENGLISH HYMN WRITERS
Compiled and Introduced by Timothy Dudley-Smith

PRAYING WITH THE ENGLISH MYSTICS
Compiled and Introduced by Jenny Robertson

PRAYING WITH THE ENGLISH POETS
Compiled and Introduced by Ruth Etchells

PRAYING WITH THE ENGLISH TRADITION
Foreword by Robert Runcie

PRAYING WITH THE MARTYRS
Preface by Madeleine L'Engle

PRAYING WITH JOHN DONNE AND
GEORGE HERBERT
Introduction by Richard Harries